The Sun Of Youth

Selected Poems Of Daisaku Ikeda

Daisaku Ikeda

EasyRead Large

Copyright Page from the Original Book

Published by World Tribune Press
a division of the SGI-USA
606 Wilshire Blvd.
Santa Monica, CA 90401

Cover and interior design by Lightbourne, Inc.

ISBN: 978-1-935523-99-4
LCCN: 2016937230

10 9 8 7 6 5 4 3 2 1

TABLE OF CONTENTS

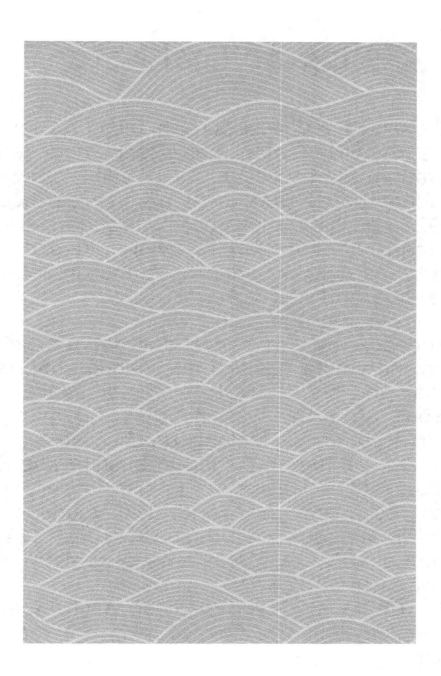

Biographical Note

Daisaku Ikeda was born in Tokyo on January 2, 1928. His family had been engaged in cultivating and harvesting *nori* (edible seaweed) for generations. Due to a massive earthquake in 1923 and his father becoming bedridden with rheumatism, the family was plunged into poverty. As a sickly child, he found great solace in reading and literature.

His older brother died while serving in the Japanese army, an event that helped solidify within the young Daisaku his lifelong abhorrence for war and his desire to work for peace.

Soon after the war, he met the man who would become his lifelong teacher, Josei Toda. Mr. Toda was then engaged in building the Soka Gakkai with a desire to banish misery from Japan, Asia, and the world. The younger man joined in Mr. Toda's effort and was instrumental in the Soka Gakkai's phenomenal growth in the postwar years.

In 1960, Mr. Ikeda succeeded Mr. Toda as the president of the Soka Gakkai, immediately embarking on various travels to spread Nichiren Buddhist teachings throughout the world. The Soka Gakkai now has members in nearly every country in the world.

Spiritual leader, philosopher, essayist, poet, and peace activist, he is also the founder of several educational and research institutes, including Soka University of America.

Throughout his life, Mr. Ikeda has placed particular emphasis on fostering youth. He steadfastly believes that it is the passion and power of youth dedicated to the happiness of all that will lead us to a world of peace.

Editor's Note

Whether it was finding hope and courage in the lines of Walt Whitman as a young man after World War II or composing verse to encourage friends now when he is well into his eighties, Daisaku Ikeda has always loved poetry. In it he finds "a crystallization of the bond between individuals, between people and society, and between humanity and nature."[1]

Moreover, he has often called for a restoration of the "poetic mind." For society to flourish, he says, we must balance our reverence for the intellect and rationalism with a renewed appreciation and development of intuition and sensibility. "The poetic mind is the source of human imagination and creativity," he writes. "It imparts hope to our life on this earth, gives us dreams, and infuses us with courage; it makes possible harmony and unity and gives us the power no army can vanquish to transform our inner world from utter desolation to richness and creativity."[2]

He is especially eager that young people "inherit the vigorous spirituality of poetry"[3] so they can be the protagonists in creating this balanced and harmonious world. In hopes of supporting this aim, we have selected eleven poems to include in *The Sun of Youth.* Written from 1970 to 1999, each has been dedicated to youth.

The SGI president's hope, and ours, is "to imagine that even one line or one phrase ... might somehow touch the reader's heart and awaken him to life by indicating what to strive for and how to live."[4]

***

[1]   Sarah Wider and Daisaku Ikeda, *The Art of True Relations: Conversations on the Poetic Heart of Human Possibilities* (Cambridge, Mass.: Dialogue Path Press, 2014), 143.

[2]   Daisaku Ikeda, "A Call for the Restoration of the Poetic Mind," December 12, 1988, *World Tribune,* 3.

[3]   Wider and Ikeda, *The Art of True Relations,* 149.

[4]   Daisaku Ikeda, *Hopes and Dreams* (Santa Monica, Calif.: World Tribune Press, 1976), 12.

Song of youth

Though clouds dot the sky
and the wind blows
the sun rises again today
The eight a.m. sun of youth
holding within itself limitless power
as it spreads its light abroad, advances on
 correct course

Never deviating from its strict orbit,
beyond mansions of the sky, filling the heavens,
a king in glory
the sun advances wordless, unspeaking

Wisdom that is in fact ignorance, decline of
 culture
mechanization of man, death of philosophy
scheming authority, deceit, trickery—
is it not to dispel these
that it sends forth its golden rays
that it advances in this lordly manner?

A sculpture of men and women in their
 entanglements
a globe whose contentions never cease
a world caught in the agony of indecision and
 revolt

human existence, the brilliance of its life all but
  extinguished
beneath the machinery of oppression—
the sun advances through the heavens
drawing forth a new vitality

The Buddhism of Nichiren is like the sun
our faith too shall be the sun
To give true proof of regeneration
filled with inner anger we advance
upon the great road of reason, sincerity, and
  wisdom

At last we have come to recognize it—
the challenge to become a true human being
It is the fight for the human revolution
that begins with one individual
and swells now to a multitude of seven million

In that region, in this region,
in that office, in this family
friends fight, friends win
The delight in these open faces, rolling forth in
  countless waves,
has become a third force

Friends who walk proudly in a life of
  self-affirming joy

friends of unlimited creativity, singing of the
  culture of the common people
friends who fight bravely to transcend the
  theory of class
friends who struggle tirelessly and without end
  to give shape to the new life
friends who tread an unshakable path, in a
  glory rooted in society
friends who are victorious in the family
  revolution, who jingle the bells of good fortune

Steadfastly we advance
in the sincere and bloodless battle of the
  century
The forces of emotionalism, panic, and envy
have become three cowardly enemies
blocking the path of our lordly peace
Their jealousy
churns like sand, rages like a storm

But we will never be afraid
We bear the banners of eternal life
and we shall advance once more
We lift high the banners of revolution

Oh
the Buddhism of Nichiren is the philosophy of
  youth
Facing the strongholds of reaction and hatred

mounted on white horses
dauntlessly the columns will go forward

The curtain has opened on the second decade
Moving no longer in a line but over a broad
 surface
you work to build the towering and fruitful
culture of the twenty-first century
This will be the stage upon which you perform!
This will be your debut!

I have my mission which is mine alone
You too
have a mission which only you can fulfill

Without the strength of youthful activity
what can the older generation accomplish?
Upon the slope of construction, from
 incompletion to completion
with songs of youth
melodies of culture
sounding the gongs of innovation
heroically, rain-battered, let us work on
With bright eyes
soft smiles
brawny muscles
red-cheeked, clean-browed
tenacious in individuality

clad in the work clothes of steadfast
 determination
you commence the construction of total
 revolution

The steel is cold and there are lashing winds
The steel is heavy—your sweat pours out

But only out of this labor and mission
will the true value of human life be born
and the music of a magnificent fruition ring
 forth

We young people will fight
Striding through the storms of meanness,
 flattery, and carping
along the road of true belief
so that a myriad flowers may bloom,
out of the valleys of darkness so that we may
 reach the high peaks of justice,
from the rigid society of our times with its sighs
to create a splendid era of human flowering
like that of Man'yoshu times
we will move forward, we will work!

The formula for the enrichment of human
 nature—
it exists nowhere but in
a complete and all-embracing faith

The profound search for a meaningful life—
it exists
in a faith that is lofty

The self-won victory over anguish—
it is none other than
the religion of the Lion King
A life unshakable in the face of strong winds—
it can be attained
only through a faith that is pure

There are difficult paths of error
mazes of mistaken belief
young people who subscribe to no theories
arrogant scholars—
But the inevitable, the finest achievement
lies in a proven religion alone

Facing the eastern sky for the morning prayer
pressing palms together solemnly
to the source of the myriad beings,
an awesome epitome of the universe in
 miniature

With this act as the point of origin for growth
 and development
in the midst of the varied forms of reality
in the midst of mankind's variety and
 complexness

like the eagle, king of creatures that soar the
 sky
like the lion, king of creatures that walk the
 earth
we advance, mounted on the winged horses of
 freedom
In our right hands gripping the profound
principles of the holy wisdom
in our left embracing the compassion of the
 Lotus, racing,
strengthening the ranks of our solidarity,
through freedom of choice and conviction, once
 more we advance

What is our goal?
It is kosen-rufu
In pursuing it we must surmount countless
 obstacles
This dedication and the long campaign to spread
 the teachings
shall be our lifelong journey

For us, there is no stopping—
we are like the flow of a mighty river
There may be those who,
beguiled by pleasant dreams, turn back alongthe
 way
There may be those who,
shunning the steep path to the peak,
blithely return to the lights of the bright city

We, though,
will go forward gallantly in the face of the
 storm
In order to build the city of Eternal Truth
bravely we will work to clear the great dense
 forest
Valiant youthful seekers of the Way
we put aside hesitant feelings, boldly push
 ahead
Without undue optimism, without sentiment
we advance ever toward the ultimate point of
 our destination

Now, along the true path, bringing Buddhism
 to society
flanking our column
many are the friends who soar aloft
In the anger-filled world of politics
in the culture of the heavenly beings
in the scholarly world of the *shomon*

there are many paths, branching many ways,
yet all come together at the rugged mountain
 of kosen-rufu
Despite skirmishes and retreats
the main body of troops never falters but
 advances in order

Laying down the foundation for the total
 revolution
our main force advances earnestly, imposingly

At times quietly observing
the movements of society
at times working in harmony with society
deeply, broadly advancing
at times advancing in fury
through the river of slander and abuse
at times, putting on the armor of endurance,
we advance to the duet of silence and dialogue
And at other times
to defend our doctrine
we risk death in a fight of pure and utter
 resistance

The progress of good health
wild dance of peace
in time to the march of the revolution of new
 life
we move

My friends!
we have been brothers from the infinite past
My friends!
we, each in our lives, are brothers and sisters
The latent bonds of comradeship that bind us
no man

no stratagems of any kind
can ever sunder

Now the curtain has fallen on one act of the
 century
Factionalism and clashing interest
egoists and trickery
shadow figures and irresponsibility
injustice and domineering authority
foul politics, visible and invisible—
can young people in their purity go along with
 these?

Only the beauty
of naturally formed solidarity
which transcends these,
the wheels that roll forward toward the
 happiness of mankind,
from these splendid wheels
these wheels that revolve with life's vitality,
from them shall come the society of the true
 human republic

Solidarity of the common people to preserve
 the dignity of life
solidarity of blood and tears that fights off every
 form of oppression
solidarity of hearts built out of idealism and
 good faith

true wheels of mankind—
though we face the criticisms of prejudice and
  ignorance
we stand tall in our pride

These worthy groups built
by men themselves, for the sake of men,
through the power of fundamental Law and the
  ultimate truth

Never playing up to authority,
never compromising with the powers of wealth,
blueprints for a great popular current
brilliant with philosophy, science, and culture—
this will be the final chapter of our human
  building

To liberate society from confrontations,
responding to all cultural demands,
a renaissance of the twenty-first century—
this we proclaim as
our great cultural movement

In the past there have been different kinds of
  revolution
political, economic, educational
But when one type of revolution is carried out
  in isolation

it lacks solidity, gives rise to strain and
 one-sidedness
A political revolution alone
calls forth bloodshed, insures no safety for the
 populace
and once again those in authority lord it over
 the masses

Likewise economic revolution
fails to fulfill the hopes of the people,
the penniless commoners are trampled underfoot
 in a process of meaningless change
A revolution in education only again is no
 blessing to the people—
it cannot bear up before the turmoil of the
 world's shifts and movements

What the people long for
to carry them through the twenty-first century
is no reorganization of external forms alone
They desire a sound revolution
carried out within themselves
gradually and in an atmosphere of peace
founded upon the philosophy and beliefs of each
 individual
This calls for farsighted judgments
and a profound system of principles

This is what I would name a total revolution

and it is this
we call kosen-rufu

If there are those who would laugh
let them laugh
if there are those who would disparage
let them disparage

For us at the end of the broad road we travel
the history of countless centuries of the future
 waits to give its proof
A monument to mankind's far-off glory and
 victory
waits for us

Dear comrades!
my beloved young people!
in this belief together we will advance with joy!

In the land of freedom
in America too
hundreds of thousands of friends are at work
In the countries of the future
on the African continent too
thousands of friends are coming to join us
In our brother lands
of Southeast Asia too
we have many friends waiting
To India too, land of neutrality

to South America, to the country of the Incas
to Australia, the island continent
the True Buddhism of the world has spread
In the countries of Europe with their age-old
 culture

we have friends who fight
In the Soviet Union, republic of the people
and finally in our neighboring land of China
friends will appear soon
Passively, actively
the world awaits us

With the ideologies
of all races, all countries
as a gateway and means of understanding,
the religious movement of renovation shall go
 forward

The support of complete knowledge
the foundation of complete democracy
the soil of a complete culture—
to complete the task of bringing these about,
Young people!
wave the banners of the world religion of
 freedom and peace

Never forget that these banners
must wave only upon foundations

that day after day are firm and unyielding

To accomplish this, young people,
I ask you today again to carry on friendly
 dialogues in the very midst of the people
My young people!
take time from your busy schedules,
listen carefully to the voice of your friend in
 trouble

because to be clear and full of confidence
like the blue sky and the sun
is what qualifies you to be glorious young
 revolutionaries
There are other banners, renowned but false
 in name—
in time their colors will fade
There are medals adorning the societies of false
 goodness
but their glow is lifeless, not a bright human
 light
There are politicians, false figures
who sooner or later will be unmasked by the
 perceptive young

There are those who see only the reality of the
 present
and those who see the eternal in the present
 reality

We choose to be the latter, and from that
standpoint
manifest ourselves, shining in glory

Fame, medals we have no use for
Simple human beings, in the palace of our flesh
we walk the pleasure-filled road of life
Along the golden road that will never crumble
for eternity
as unfamed, uncrowned human beings we walk
on

Once more, young people, my friends!

With the present century as our stairway
let us go forward toward that mountain of the
twenty-first century
stoutly, vigorously pulling our way up
we will open again the curtain
upon a new century's development

Young people!
you must go on living
Above all, you must go on living

As chief figures in the brilliant total revolution
resolutely you will achieve your victory in
history

The eight a.m. sun of youth
today again is rising!
It is rising in time to the beat of youth!

***

Written on December 5, 1970. This translation,
by Burton Watson, first appeared in *Songs from
My Heart* (fourth printing, 1997).

"Second decade" indicates the second decade
since Mr. Ikeda was inaugurated Soka Gakkai
president, on May 3, 1960.

Man'yoshu times: The period in early Japanese
history reflected in the *Man'yoshu* (The
Collection of Myriad Leaves), the earliest
anthology of Japanese poetry, compiled in the
eighth century. The poet is thinking in
particular of the Nara period (710–84), an era
of great cultural and artistic achievement.

Lion King: King of the beasts, the lion is often
employed in Buddhism to symbolize persons
or writings of the highest eminence.

shomon: Or sravaka; one who attains
enlightenment by listening to the Buddha's

teachings. He represents the seventh of the ten states of existence and is characterized as a scholar. Though some Mahayana sutras deny that the *shomon* and *engaku,* or *pratyeka-buddha* (the eighth of the ten states), can attain true Buddhahood, the Lotus Sutra insists that they can.

In the river of revolution

Along with time
the fierce river of revolution flows on
today too tomorrow again too

Young man,
you who shine with a fresh new light!
It must be you and no other,
holding fast to the image in your mind
by mountains and rivers skillfully
you must build strong embankments

Young man run!
run for the sake of the common people
run, explore the endless borders of your world
From past times sons of the revolution
with this reflection in the midst of the ultimate
 river,
what sort of course have they marked out?

convulsion of anger
thesis of grief
the cold laugh of irony
tear-filled eyes

And yet those youths who race in the vanguard

still in the face of this enticing challenge
display boundless fidelity

This perhaps is the destiny of youth
Young man, you do right,
for revolution in the end is a romance

Wanderings of the dreaming spirit, the kiss of
  romance,
upon this canvas of human life and society and
  history
leave vivid points and lines
the life of a painter who seems of surpassing
  genius—
the victory of the wisdom of the youthful
  revolutionary
lies in this one point

In the basic scriptures we read:
"The mind is like a skilled painter"
or again:
"I expound the teachings that move within one's
  own mind"
If expression be removed from the reality that
  is
man what remains?
expression expression inevitable expression
expression that cannot be avoided no
  matterwhat—

reveling in this splendid freedom
Mishima cried out, Dazai died

They wanted to give expression perhaps
even to their own demise
But in the art you strive for
there is no need for such narcissism
Basic, inherent expression—
this is enough,
for this is the beauty toward which human truth
 gravitates

It does not matter if no one sees it
You do not need to lean on anyone
but following in accord with the single Dharma,
having faith in the true nature of your life
and the greatness of the shining victory of the
 Human Party
rapturously confidently dance your way along

We have no need of any sect
Valorously transcending the obstacles
of narrow partisanship, of cliques,
as human beings
as stark-naked human beings,
live, move, and for the sake of the joyous new
 society
fight, young man!
And I too will fight!

The sect of nonsectarianism
the sect called human being, which is no sect
 at all—
let us call this the Human Party

People perhaps may laugh
the arrogant men of power will ignore us
men of cold intellect will reject the concept

But do not grieve, friend!
They could never understand the "Human
 Party,"
for men drowned in the drunkenness of pride
 and arrogance and ignorance,
no image of the self
can be cast in the mirror

Do men's selves, existing only vaguely,
have so much as a fragment of compassion for
 the masses?
There is only barren desert there
When the light of the life force has become
 parched and dried up
it can never shine through
the shrouding mists of the world
and no clear and certain road to the future
can ever be revealed

But when you stand

upon that silent, artless, and unfathomable
 Dharma,
the solemn essence
that flows beneath the *Sein* of
the universe, the world, and human life,
then for the first time that clouded mirror
 hidden within you
will shine, be wiped clean,
and reflect the true image of you yourselves

Young man,
you are a youthful sage who has grasped this!
The ultimate world that
Goethe
Pascal
Einstein
only imperfectly glimpsed—
you are its perceiver

There is no one stronger than you
no one more trustworthy
You wear no crown perhaps
but your crownlessness should be your joy

For the overflowing power of the human being
 who holds this wisdom,
conferring no power, no wealth, no medals,
like an ultimate point of arrival—
in the depths of your heart

you embody it

Ah, human being
this unadorned reality
this upright existence
this sturdy essence that never falters or fades

Young man!
this human shout of joy,
so eloquent, so strong, so beautiful—
in the end and always you must salute it
 gravely,
for in it alone are the principles, the sole
 human likeness
of the revolutionary expression which you would
 fashion

And here too
in the revolutionary throb of the revolution
the revolution, in art that expands in a
 thousand, ten thousand waves,
the sublime experiment exists here, I believe
And here alone will the light that comes with
 the
manifestation of the revolution of wisdom
 appear

Flowing from its springs
the joyful life of revolution

making flowers of awakening bloom out of
 anguish,
the springtime of revolution—
these in their pure, strong gladness
are the days of the revolution

In the youthful heart, so long sought for,
the tidal waves of excitement and elation—
when they surge forth from this shore to that
then the eternally flowing river of the revolution
will change into a magnificent torrent
This will be the society no one has ever seen
 before
the homeland that everyone has sought

Then men for the first time
will emerge from the shiftings of the dark night
to return to themselves
and mankind too
will reach the oasis, reversion to the primal

And you who,
in the midst of the river of revolution that
 moves toward the twenty-first century,
grip the rudders of sagacity and justice,
it will be your skill that brings this about

∗∗∗

Written on September 5, 1971. This translation, by Burton Watson, first appeared in *Songs from My Heart* (1978).

Yukio Mishima (1925–70): A novelist and playwright who committed ritual suicide after failing in an attempt to enlist support for his right-wing ideology.

Osamu Dazai (1909–48): An influential novelist who committed suicide by drowning.

Sein: German for "existence."

Angels of peace

Angels of peace, you bearers of culture!
Ah, the fervent breath
of my friends on fife and drum—
you fashion a single ever-fresh flower
dressing up our dreary world.

Marching to the flanks, or forward,or
 pinwheeling
at the drum major's bidding,
the elegance of close-order drill
creates a divinely fluid dance flowing from the
 fervor
that charges your minds, charges your bodies.

Along the chilly paths of discipline
in our chaotic and jaded age,
your radiant circle (a ring of life linked with
 precious life)
emits the sparkling good sense of youth
and a well-wrought song of triumph.

Daughters of the nameless masses,
pioneers in smashing the walls between people
as you melt the seasoned ices of ideology,
you are the unofficial envoys—
true and trustworthy angels of peace.

Strangers to political craft,
strangers to diplomatic strategems,
without speaking a word, you spread our
 philosophy of peace,
you extend the frontiers of friendship—
touching the people where they are.

Using neither bullets nor bayonets,
but only simple fifes and drums,
you play the basic rhythms of the Mystic
 Universe;
none can help responding from deep within.
Certainly you shall spur the world to peace!

Yes, we find in you a florid oasis
greening our spiritual desert:
your lighthearted "Do Re Mi"
your lyrical and lucid "Moon Over a Ruined
 Castle,"
your "Symphony of Joy."

I shall never forget
tears gleaming in the eyes of those angels
who see from afar the bulwarks of world
 solidarity
beyond the soaring horizon.
I cheer the tunes in every glistening pearly
 tear.

As you evade the flames of war,
clearing the din of progress
and announcing to all the New Truth,
you light now one, now another
light of life among us.

The lights you've lit merge into patterns
spreading everywhere over the gloom,
over the ugliness of these latter days;
your light soon will generate the passion
to fire all our tomorrows.

***

Written on September 18, 1971. This
translation, by Robert Epp, first appeared in
Hopes and Dreams (1976).

This poem was written to the young women's
fife and drum corps of the Soka Gakkai. Mr.
Ikeda initiated this group, as well as the brass
band for young men, in 1956. They perform
worldwide in parades and culture festivals.

"Moon Over a Ruined Castle," a popular
Japanese song that is a favorite of the author.

The people

Like the surging of a vast sea
stretching to the far horizon—the people

Joy, sorrow descending on them
in roaring torrents, yet each day making some
 little joke,
going their way together, living on—the people
From the beginning
there's been nothing to surpass the strength
 and shout of the people
from the beginning
nothing to outrun the pace of the people's
 wisdom
from the beginning
nothing to rival the banners of the people's
 justice

Yet in the past
and today as well
the history of the people and their struggle
has been bathed in tears of suffering and want

A poet put it this way:
"While ignorance and misery remain on earth
we will never give up our fight!"

You dark wielders of power,
can you not hear the lonely sighs
of the people troubled and sickened by you?
Wise ones of the world,
can you not perceive
that a single atom
is bursting with the laws of the entire universe?
Are the masses in their long and distant
 wanderings
only meek, subservient objects in your sight?

"The people"—
it is a word I love
People!
why do you believe
it is your fate
solely to still the storm of the heart
and be crushed beneath the stones of tyranny?

Why do you not
cast off your ancient chains?
Have you not the right to emerge from the
 history of the dead,
to become heroes of the history of the living?

Blood that has flowed cannot be redeemed
tears that have been shed are beyond recall
Ah, but
do not be silent!

You must not resign yourselves!
You must not grow weary!
To put an end to the refrain of this stupid
 history
dominated by a handful of men in power,
to silence once for all this pitiful weeping,
in dancing waves of people,
for the sake of the people of the future
you must gain victory!

Now is the time
to ring down the curtain on this rainbow farce
played out by elder statesmen with their plots
 for power,
the generals rattling their sabers,
the glittering rich and mighty alone
You, looking up to the skies,
roaming the earth,
will be the leading actors on the stage now,
creating as you go a wholly different drama of
 history

People!
you alone are reality
Outside of you there is no real world

The age will not forget to wait and pray
for the true movement of the people

It will not forget that you alone
are the great sea into which all things flow,
the furnace, the crucible in which all things,
emerging from chaos, are refined
for the sake of a new birth,
and you are the touchstone
to distinguish truth from falsity in all things

Science, philosophy
art, religion,
all undertakings
must be directed toward the people

Science without you is coldhearted
philosophy without you is barren
art without you is empty
religion without you is merciless

You should look down on those who sneer at
 you,
not be bound by those who analyze and judge
 others coldly,
ignore those who hate the earthy smell about
 you

You who work away in silence,
you with your strong muscles, browned by the
 sun—
I can hear the pure, rapid beating

of the heart in your breast

I will spend my life exerting myself for your
 sake
Though at first sight I seem to stand in
 isolation,
I want to make it my proud and only mission
to fight on and on for you alone,
always in your behalf

I will fight,
you will fight,
fight until the day when,
on this earth,
your rough hands will tremble
and the joy of life shines forth in your simple
 faces

I will fight!
You must fight too!
Wherever you may be,
holding fast to a steady tempo
today again I fight!

***

Presented to the members of the Soka Gakkai
 young women's division on September 28,

1971. This translation, by Burton Watson, first appeared in *Songs from My Heart* (1978).

Weeds

They live
rank on rank of them in their green nakedness
they live vigorously
never flinching from the autumn frost,
 unbending in will,
through the supple resilience that is their
 heaven-given nature
they live on in joy

They live greedily they live
never the least air of gloom about them
to the life-giving springs of the great earth their
 mother
calling out in answer
multiplying their friends as they live on
In the light of the heavens they live
 discordantly
giving thanks to the dews and springs of the
 earth
they live serenely

Sternly they battle with their surroundings
freely they take delight in their surroundings
day by day they carve out a life of fullness
with the drought, the gale, the drenching rain,

the morning dew, the sunset, the stars that fill
 the sky
they live on, dancing and singing

The burning heat relentlessly torments them,
the parching dryness, when one drop of water
 is a precious pearl,
the desperate fight—
The sudden storm in its madness would destroy
 them
but though they sway and bend to the ground
their chests swell with pride

The squalls attack, washing them, trying to
 down them,
but though their front ranks, their rear ranks
 are swamped,
unenraged they pick themselves up from the
 water

Waves of ordeal are never easy to bear
Sustained endurance in the face of life and
 death,
the unfaltering resistance that alone conquers
 all,
they who know no surrender
they who exude a thriving vitality
and they whose smiling faces never change—
even deserts are a waterside to them

even foul mud is an oasis
even barren fields are a longed-for paradise

And at last there comes to them
a time of rest

Morning dews gently call them to waking
little birds beat drums in the sky
and the light of the sun fills the grassy fields

The crimson setting sun colors them,
from the far edge of the horizon bidding them
 farewell,
praising them for their day's labor
and they, sitting straight up, sink into
 meditation

The Milky Way as is it flows down the sky
speaks to them each night of dreams,
grieving over the impermanence and misfortune
of history's thousand changes, the ten thousand
 transformations of life

Who is aware of the awakening
of these tiny lives?
Who salutes them from the heart?

They know nothing of hothouses

they would not wish for the tedium of the
 potted plant
no thoughts of flower shows occupy them
They go unadmired
unpicked—
needless to say no one would buy them
But listen
to their untroubled soliloquy
to their intense confidence and pride!

"All artifice, all human skill,
seen in the light of the highest value, which is
 to live,
are mere phantoms!"
that I know is what they say to one another
 as they tremble and sway

"Such elaborate protection
such delicate love
we have no need for"

"We do not fear the gale
we do not grieve at isolation
or resent our fate"

"We leave the nightingale to his plum tree
leave the moon to lodge in the pine
to the willow we leave the spring showers"

"For the nameless
there the mission and the flowering of the
 nameless
for the wild, that which belongs to the wild
With our own hands
we will open up our own road
This is the beautiful road
of our green existence"

In a theater where there is no applause
endlessly, earnestly they go on giving
 expression
to the beauty of their gratuitous revels and
 parades
Ah, there name is "weeds"

How great you are
How sturdy you are
How merry you are

Green friends, who live wholehearted
come here!
let me share my seat with you

I will watch steadily over your trials
I alone am moved to praise your vigorous truth
I want your form to be
the guideline that governs my whole life

Gazing upward at the flowing stars,
live in your own free way!
If that be the proper path,
then with the elements of your true nature just
 as they are
keep on forever living as you have lived

Beauty of gregariousness
strength of the indigenous
wisdom that adapts itself to circumstance

This is the unadorned world of the common
 people
the republican world of the human tribe
this indeed is the yearned-for world of the
 Serene Light

In this sky and earth from antiquity
endlessly following the rainbow,
as though sprung up from the earth,
the vigor of life!

The weeds, immersed in joy,
today again live their lives
vigorously attaining to a love that is equal, they
 live
in ranks, forgetting ascetic practices,
today again they live through their lives!

***

Presented to the members of the Soka Gakkai young men's division on October 3, 1971. This translation, by Burton Watson, first appeared in *Songs from My Heart* (1978).

The truth of Melos

Surmounting the cliffs that rise up steeply,
tramping the vast plains of the sky,
threading through dark forests,
racing ever onward, the young man Melos

He runs, that is all—
to fulfill the firm-binding vow made withhis
 friend,
to give proof of the quality of trustworthiness
holding fast to the highest purity of heart, he
 runs on

He does not see the green trees,
he forgets the lively streets of town,
never looking up at the silver clouds,
like the dark wind he runs on

He strides forward through the midst of river
 waves
Clothed in robes of Truth,
praying to some great entity
whose eminence he does not understand,
he does nothing but run on and on

It is a race toward his death in the world

it is a race toward eternal rebirth

Young Melos!
You turned from the world of men,
full of falsehood and delusion,
to a rare and certain reality,
the loftiest, most beautiful, most clean

You have left behind a melody of Truth that
 will echo forever
as long as mankind shall exist

That strong Truth, wherein did it lie?
Was it in the bodily strength with which you
 swam the muddy current?
Was it in the valor with which you struck down
 the mountain robbers?

No!
for none of these penetrates to the true essence
It was in the supremacy that lies within your
 own heart
with which you conquered, fierce as they were,
those nightmares of fatigue that for a moment
 invaded your breast,

longings for your fond homeland,
attachments to the warmth of family,

most evil enemies within you that for a time
  overwhelmed
this brave man who otherwise would bow to
  nothing—
at that time, I know,
you must have acknowledged your frustrations
and held parley
with those deluding dreams within your heart
that secretly tempted you to pleasure and
  delight

But Melos rose up
for Melos had the passion of a youth
who burns for justice,
that transcends the sweet lure of vast dream
  fancies
He won out,
won out over himself
From past times, when the path of the convert
is threatened by bonds of affection shallow but
  hard to cut,
or the fear of pains too sharp to bear
and he retreats a step in despair,
then comes the logic of self-justification
that leads him to retreat still further

I have no desire
to scoff at such weakness,
to make fun of longing,
to chastise fear

It is all right if no one joins me
Observing all things objectively,
sitting upright in deep and calm thought
I would fix my eyes upon my own mission
and join the ranks of those who fight in the
 cause of justice

But this I would say—
in the idle ease of one who has cast off friends
there is a pain of remorse that will last until
 the end of life
Rather than live sorrowing in some nook or
 corner
forcing lonely smiles,
I would rather elect to die for Truth

One person is enough, someone who will resist
 this avalanche that swallows all before it
For if no one resists it,
then Truth will continue forever to face defeat
and history will become a procession of fancies
 and falsehoods

I would remember this:
"Only the race of truly great valor
can destroy the obsessions of suspicion and
 scheming
and bring about the ultimate flowering of human
 truth"

***

Written on October 31, 1971. This translation, by Burton Watson, first appeared in *Songs from My Heart* (1978).

The poem is based on "Run, Melos!," a short story by Osamu Dazai (1909–48), a postwar novelist who killed himself. "Run, Melos!" deals with the Greek legend of Damon and Pythias, the latter here called Melos. The youth Melos, having angered the tyrant Dionysius and been condemned to death, was allowed to return home to tend to his younger sister's wedding on condition that his best friend be held as a hostage in his place. The poem depicts Melos's struggle to overcome various obstacles and return to the tyrant's court by the appointed time so that his friend will not be executed in his place. According to the legend, he succeeded in doing so and the tyrant, deeply impressed with his fidelity and sense of honor, pardoned him.

To my beloved young American friends—youthful Bodhisattvas of the Earth

Dedicated to the American youth division members at a U.S.-Japan Goodwill Exchange Meeting in New York

The world today is ailing.
This continental land, America,
is also faltering, about to succumb
to the same illness.

In the past, the land of America,
was a symbol of freedom and democracy—
fresh new focus of the world's hopes.

You! Young people
who uphold the Mystic Law!
You! Youthful Bodhisattvas of the Earth,
dedicated to the attainment
of kosen-rufu!

You have chosen this time
to stand resolutely
on this grand stage
as the curtain majestically lifts,
as we strive to transform
a century verging on barrenness
into a new era of life—
the twenty-first century!

You, more than anyone,
are the noble emissaries of the Buddha.
Cherishing the values
of compassion, wisdom, and justice,
you are endowed with the mission
to lead lives of eloquence, poetry,
culture, and philosophy,
to dance and stride unfettered
with vigor and with grace.

Those who have awakened
to their mission are strong.
Your mission is to show to all
the goal of kosen-rufu,
the clear and certain means
to realize peace and happiness
for humankind;
to construct within your hearts
palaces of human dignity.
This is the mission of those
who have embraced truth

eternal and universal.

The mission you possess
is vast and noble—
You who have awakened to the Mystic Law,
this infinitely precious, indestructible,
eternal, and boundless Law.

You! Youth of America
who have begun the
steady advance
of your daily lives,
as you take up the challenge
to work toward kosen-rufu.

With a roar,
valiant and ceaseless,
proclaim to society
the absolute values
of peace and culture,
as you advance
step by step,
as you progress
stage by stage.

Now is the time
once more to construct
a land of unshakable joy and prosperity,
fresh with the love of humanity,

here in America,
this beloved land of freedom,
where people have gathered
from throughout the world
seeking the fulfillment of their dreams.

You!
Champions who struggle courageously
for the sake of the Mystic Law,
yours is the responsibility
to guide the entire world
to the flower garden
of safety and tranquillity.
Chanting the Mystic Law
with resonant, resounding voices,
plant your feet on the earth of society;
sink in your roots,
bring forth flowers and blossoms,
as you continue to speak,
to converse, to call from the heart,
to move and meet—
for this friend here
for that friend there
for the people of this city,
for friends far away.

Singing with joy
you gather under the banner
of the Great Law,
of teachings correct and true.

Create and complete
for yourself and with others
wondrous lives
of eternity, happiness, true self, and purity.

America, this land uniting nations,
where people from everywhere
have gathered in harmony,
a miniature of the entire world.
Only in the unity and solidarity of
so many diverse peoples
is to be found the principle and formula
for global peace.

You whom I trust and love,
grounding yourselves on the
fundament of the Mystic Law,
hold aloft once more
the symbol and significance of
those stars and stripes as they
stream and ripple in the wind.
Never forget your vow,
made in the infinite past,
to love this homeland,
to stand alone against injustice
as vibrant youth of high ideals,
undertaking the adventure
and battle for human advancement.

You!
Wise and passionate youth
who know deeply,
and share with others
the true purpose of life,
life's true aspect—
the three thousand realms
contained in a single life moment.
As you live out your lives,
never forget the infinite dignity
of your mission as pioneers
of the movement for kosen-rufu,
to create an enduring and perfect peace.

Youth!
Compassionate and committed,
your faith flows ceaselessly like water
pure and powerful—
strong, yet gentle.
Over the long course of history,
your lives are destined to shine
with victory, the grateful praise
of future generations.
Now is the time
for us to join together
—you and I and our friends—
to enjoy the beautiful, precious bonds,
the deepest dimension of our shared humanity,
to expand this golden circle
into the coming century.

You! Young people
living now and into the future!
You who advance,
who never lose sight
of the single point
of our clear and certain goal,
however opinions may differ.

Today again study!
Today again take action!
Today again strive!
Pace today's meaningful progress,
tomorrow, advance another cheerful step.
Each day fusing your life
with the sublime Mystic Law,
wipe the sweat from your brow
as you ascend the hill of completion
toward the summit of priceless self-perfection.
Be as the lotus flower
blooming pure amidst the
muddied realities of society.

Faith is—
to fear nothing
to stand unswayed
the power to surmount any obstacle.
Faith is the source from which
all solutions flow.
Faith is the engine that propels us
in the thrilling voyage of life,

a life victorious and transcendent.

You who shoulder America's future!
Recalling, learning from
the assaults borne by the Daishonin,
never fear the persecutions that will
inevitably arise as kosen-rufu unfolds.
Never become base or cowardly!
Never be taken in by the false
and cunning words
of those who have betrayed
their faith.

Working for the sake of the Law
for the happiness of people
become the very essence of conviction,
bring new light to
the hearts and lives of many.

You! Successors to the task of kosen-rufu!
The twenty-first century is at hand.
Correctly develop
your remarkable abilities and powers—
for the sake of the American continent,
for the sake of this troubled, unstable world.
First, you yourself
must realize all
your dreams and desires;
savor a profound and satisfying life,

free from all regret;
advance again with exalted step;
with unshakable confidence, create
a golden history of cause and effect.

Youthful friends and comrades
swirling out onto the grand stage
of the twenty-first century!
Not a single one of you
should fall behind.
When you who have gathered now
take your places on society's stage
the waves of kosen-rufu
will further rise and further swell.
In my ears resounds
the applause of trust and respect
as I picture my friends
—the members of SGI-USA—
joining hands,
turning smiling faces
toward one another.

With complete faith in you
as successors,
I entrust to you
the entire endeavor of kosen-rufu
and can
therefore proceed
to every corner of the earth!
Confident that

from this yet narrow path
you will forge a grand passage
into the future,
I am happy and filled with joy.

New York
June 20, 1981

Youth, scale the mountain of kosen-rufu of the twenty-first century

A renowned mountaineer
when asked his reasons for climbing,
said of the mountain:
"Because it is there!"

We are now climbing
the mountain of the twenty-first century,
the mountain of kosen-rufu!

Beloved youth!
Holding aloft the banner
of the correct teaching of the Mystic Law,
bravely scale the mountain
of the twenty-first century,
in this way establishing a truly
autonomous and satisfying
way of life.

To this end,
continue to ascend

step by step, one by one,
the mountains large and small
that rise before us each day.
For the value of a deeply fulfilling youth
can only be found within those
who strive to surmount
the harsh realities
of their own lives and of society!
Only when you dedicate yourself
to pursuing this path
of your own profound choosing
can you develop,
with quiet strength,
a sense of self
inexpressibly expansive
like vast, unbounded plains.
Only then can you live out
the entirety of your life
with unshakable confidence!

Young people who are my disciples!
Live on—
for the cause of the Great Law
that is eternal, absolute, and indestructible!
Live on—
to accomplish the noble mission
for which you were born!
Live on—
to ring the bell of peace in the world
and raise the flag of justice in society,

the goals which are our creed!

Again today, the sun rises.
It rises majestically—
in the morning of spring cherry blossoms,
in the burning heat of summer days,
in the autumn of red-gold leaves,
despite brooding skies and blowing snows.
Together with the sun,
let us be bold!
My friends, heirs to the future,
live your youth so that the sun,
refulgent with the Great Law,
rises ceaselessly, steadily,
in your hearts!

My young friends!
Youth is another name for the sun.
Embracing the sun of infinite possibilities,
may you make today
victorious in every way!

It is more than seven hundred years
since the Buddhism of the sun arose.
And now, in accordance with the teaching
"The farther the source, the longer the stream,"
a great, exuberant tide has flowed and spread
throughout the world.

A half century has passed
since the founding, in 1951,
of the Soka Gakkai youth division,
committed to kosen-rufu—
people of courage and conviction
holding high the banner of
the Buddhism of the sun.
At that time,
some two hundred sixty youth
—gallant young men
and purehearted young women—
gathered with indomitable determination.

Over the course of five decades,
the flow to which they gave rise
has continued to gather strength.
At times its waters
have piled up on
massive rocks;
at times they have risen
in response to storms and downpours;
at times they have receded
beneath the scorching heat.
Yet today this flow has grown
into a grand and vibrant current
of five million young people,
a sustaining force for Japanese society.
Please remember—
the authentic successors to the
Soka Gakkai founding presidents

have all been members
of the youth division.

No one has the power to stop
this majestic and mighty flow!
It will continue to surge on
toward the ocean
growing ever deeper,
ever wider along the way.
It rushes to the forefront of the era,
unimpeded by whatever forces
of authority or sinister obstruction
are mustered against it.

Thanks to the brave and vigorous
efforts of youth,
Nichiren Daishonin's Buddhism of the sun
has come to shine beyond Japan
to illuminate the entire world.
This mighty current
of people practicing the Mystic Law
now flows in
one hundred twenty-eight countries.
As an unparalleled global expression
of the Buddha's Dharma,
it flows jubilantly and eternally
for peace, for the dignity of life,
imparting compassion
in every imaginable form.

It has always been young people
who have led the way in these efforts!
The Daishonin declares:

> If Nichiren's compassion
> is truly great and encompassing,
> Nam-myoho-renge-kyo will spread
> for ten thousand years and more,
> for all eternity.

Our well-ordered procession
of compassion and philosophy,
committed to protecting religious freedom,
has no class distinctions,
or national borders.
We advance so that
each individual may realize
the mission, rights, and happiness
that are inalienably theirs.

We absolutely oppose violence!
We absolutely oppose war!
Grounded in these great Buddhist teachings,
gaining the support of advocates
of culture and peace,
we cause expanding circles
of empathy to flower—
beyond borders
across ideological differences.

Because everyone
has the right to become happy.

I eagerly await your growth.
I pray for it with all my heart.
For I know that this
is the only way that
kosen-rufu will advance.
Therefore I say to you:
Never forget that our daily practice
—reciting sutra passages and chanting
 daimoku—
is the force to propel your ascent
of the challenging mountain of
the twenty-first century
as it rises before you.

"If a person cannot manage
to cross a moat ten feet wide,
how can he cross one that is
a hundred or two hundred feet?"
True to this teaching
you must win, no matter what,
in the place where you find yourself
at this moment!
No one can fail to respect
and be moved by a person
who chants daimoku with all their might.
For daimoku is the very essence
of the Daishonin's Buddhism!

My young friends!
Always bear in mind
the spirit of this passage!
Put it into action,
courageously and wholeheartedly!
Never lose hope
no matter how painful your situation!
Hope is the source of
infinite strength.
To have hope is to have faith!

Human beings possess
unique dignity and value.
They alone have the ability
to generate hope from within.
Over the course of life,
you may at times
appear beaten down.
But never be defeated
in the realm of faith.
So long as your faith
remains unyielding,
convincing proof of victory
invariably awaits!
That proof will be made evident
to all in society.
For the Buddhism you uphold
embodies the principle that
the three thousand realms
of the phenomenal world

are encompassed in a single life moment.

Young friends
who will live on in the new century!
Grow as leaders
of insight and understanding,
never forgetting to walk
alongside the people.
For the people are sovereign,
and the history of the world
has always borne out their wisdom.

As long as our efforts
enjoy the support of the people
and we maintain faith,
we will continue to advance
limitlessly, enduringly
into history.

Therefore, my young friends,
have pride in the many difficult labors
you have taken on,
become guides and examples
for a life as good citizens.
Consider it your highest honor
to be youthful philosophers of action!

We know that the new century
will require the emergence

of outstanding young leaders.
Those who have
neither faith nor philosophy
are like compassless ships!
The times are in motion,
steadily, inexorably shifting
from an era of materialism
to an age of abstract ideas,
from an age of ideas
to an era focused
on the inner reality of life.
People have begun to see
that the values that bring
authentic happiness
are only to be found within life itself.

Today what matters
is neither popularity, fame, nor wealth.
In their wisdom,
the people extend their respect
and seek expectantly for leaders
of genuine human greatness.

In this age of the common people,
the real leaders are those
who have won the people's trust.
We are all equal,
no one is superior or inferior.
My young friends,
I hope each of you

as leaders for the new century
will remain engaged with the people
day in and day out,
living among them,
communicating warmly,
resonantly sharing their concerns,
always breathing
in rhythm with their lives.

I have faith in you!
I cherish high expectations for you!
Without you
kosen-rufu will not be realized!

Enduring every manner
of persecution,
I, too, as a disciple of Josei Toda,
whom I chose as my mentor in life,
have striven to advance
the cause of the people,
the cause of the Mystic Law.
This is the goal I pledged
with my mentor and fellow members
to achieve!
And I declare here
my utter confidence
that all baseless calumnies
will meet with the strict, just
judgment of history.

Where a single, determined individual
has stood up to all the harassment
that power and authority
can bring to bear,
there the triumphant banner
of human revolution
will ripple forever
high in the sky!

My friends,
I urge you—
Never give in to base instincts!
Never be cowardly!
Never betray the trust of others!
For the hearts of such people
are sordid and degenerate.
However high-sounding their rhetoric
they in fact dwell in the realms
of all-consuming desire
and blind animal instinct.

Young leaders!
Direct penetrating insight
to perceive the essential nature
of every issue and incident!
Clearly expose the vicious intent
at the root of the challenges
confronted as we strive
to spread the Mystic Law!

Young champions of the future!
Be people of wisdom!
Be a revolutionizing force!
Do not be foolish!
Never allow yourself to be deceived!
Develop discernment!
These are the requisites of faith—
as the Daishonin states:
"When the skies are clear,
the ground is illuminated."

At its essence
Buddhism is a struggle
between the forces of happiness and misery,
between justice and iniquity,
between the Buddha
and the demonic forces of destruction!
Please recognize this
deeply and firmly
as the reality of your own life.

My young friends,
pass victoriously
over those sad comrades
who abandoned our once-shared faith.
Associate with people who seek the truth
who actively embody
the Treasure Tower in their lives.
Time and again
turn the wheels,

revolve the spheres
of our great movement
grounded in Buddhism.

To lead a life richly meaningful
we require a profound philosophy
in which to place faith.
There is no greater glory
than to embrace this magnificent
Buddhism of the sun
as you live out your youth
with passion and joy!
Here is found
the very essence of youth!

The mountain of the twenty-first century
looms before us!
It is already within sight!
This new century belongs to you!
This is your dawn!
This is your time to shine!
This is the grand stage on which to realize
your fullest potential
and further solidify
all that you have achieved!

May 3, 2001—
Let us aim for that glorious day
when we together reach the summit!

Remember that our struggles
up to that moment
will determine the outcome
of the current phase of kosen-rufu.
My young friends
possessing profound mission!
Aiming for that day,
continue to exert yourselves
in your Buddhist practice
with light and cheerful step!
Give your all each day
in health and high spirits!

All of your exertions
are for your own benefit.
They are for the sake of the people,
for friends who struggle and suffer.
Know that this is the voyage of youth
dedicated to all that is good and just.

Write the magnificent history
of your own life
inscribing it in eternity!
Bold, sustained, and energetic efforts
are the only way to do this!
When you confront suffering,
when the way forward seems blocked,
muster courage, dauntless courage!
Remember the many comrades
who believe in you

and in whom you can believe!
Seniors in faith everywhere
await your success!
Fellow members
eagerly follow your efforts!
These comrades are to be found
throughout the entire world!
More than anything, chant daimoku
in order to master
and triumph over yourself!
Do not spare your voice!
Speak out clearly
with the force of a lion's roar!

Remember also
that all of your actions and endeavors
are unmistakably witnessed
by the original Buddha
who surveys the three existences of
past, present, and future,
the original Buddha who assures us
that all the benevolent forces
of nature and life
will extend their protection
to the heroes of kosen-rufu.
To have this confidence
is to have faith!

Never fear the slights, insults,
or scornful criticism of others!

Such travails are nothing
compared to those of Shakyamuni,
much less the great persecutions
that beset Nichiren Daishonin!
It is only natural
that we should encounter
buffeting winds of opposition,
as proof that we are living
in full accord with the
Daishonin's teachings.
We should consider this
our defining honor.

Nobel young successors!
Cherish your venerable parents,
treasure human society.
And realize with pride
that the Buddhist principle
of the white lotus blooming
in muddy waters
applies to the
demanding, swamp-like
realities of human society.
Life in the real world is complicated,
full of contradictions.
But I urge you, young successors,
to confidently fight your way
into the magnificent inner palace
of your life!
Know that limitless happiness and peace

are to be found within
your own heart!

Sometimes you may have to wait,
patiently enduring!
At times, strike out boldly
to secure a stunning victory!
This day will never come again.
Therefore advance undeterred
today and every day.
This is the life of a bodhisattva
emerging from the earth.

Faith means to fear nothing,
to make yourself an eternal victor!
It is found in actions that give rise
to persons of outstanding humanity
who manifest the underlying unity of
people, society, and the Buddhist Law.
Society is harsh—
do not be complacent,
do not let yourself be swept away
by the worlds' ever-changing tides!
Remember that you are the protagonists,
proud authors of your own history!
Do not be misled by superficial appearances!
If you allow yourself to be swayed
by the "eight winds"
of others' praise or censure,
you will have led yourself to sad defeat.

My dear young friends!
You must be victorious in life!

Young disciples
whose growth is my incessant prayer!
Now once more
come together in united striving
as you press forward
on this great unending path!
Advance cheerfully and spiritedly
singing well-loved Gakkai songs—
"The Song of the Crimson Dawn"
"The Song of Indomitable Dignity"!
Countless young successors
follow in your footsteps.
Let us share the struggle
of ascending the adamantine peak
of the twenty-first century!

When you reach the summit,
all the world
that unfolds before you
will be yours.
There is no higher path in life
than this—of a youth devoted
to joyous and
infinitely satisfying struggle
on behalf of the Buddhist Law.
Knowing this,
I entrust everything to you!

***

Composed in Oita Prefecture, Kyushu, Japan, on December 10, 1981, and presented to the members of the Soka Gakkai youth division. This English translation, by the Soka Gakkai, is based on the version with subsequent revisions made by the author in 1999 and first appeared in *Journey of Life* (2014).

"The farther the source": Nichiren, *The Writings of Nichiren Daishonin,* vol.1., 736.

one hundred twenty-eight countries: As 2016, the SGI is in 192 countries and territories.

"If Nichiren's compassion": WND-1, 736.

"If a person cannot manage": WND-1, 766.

"When the skies are clear": WND-1, 376.

May 3: Designated "Soka Gakkai Day." May 3 is the anniversary of the inauguration of the Soka Gakkai's second and third presidents in 1951 and 1960, respectively. It is often used

as a target date for advancing the movement
of kosen-rufu.

A blue deeper than indigo itself

To my young friends on kosen-rufu day

The new day belongs to youth,
Fresh and bracing, like the green wheat
 fieldsshining with morning frost.

Though already in March,
the cold was yet fierce
on Mount Fuji at dawn.
At the call which came
as sudden as a flash of lightning,
six thousand young
Bodhisattvas of the Earth
hastened to come together in high spirits.

With their breath puffing white,
and their footsteps sounding in the dim woods,
they crossed the still-sleeping land.

Young girls with rosy cheeks
and young boys dressed for school—
all stood tall,
though wearing little warm clothing.

In the chill darkness
their eyes shone all the more bright—
fired with the certain beat
of the coming of a great moment at the break
 of morn.

Ah, the freshness of youth called out
beautifully and powerfully,
heralding the rise of a brilliant new sun.

O March 16,
day of endless import.

On that day,
under our mentor, Josei Toda,
we made up a mini-model of kosen-rufu;
and on that day,
mentor and disciple swore to strike out for their
 common cause.
This pledge will go on for all time.

This day of deep meaning
is called Kosen-rufu Day.

When this century's greatest battle had gone
 by—
a bitter storm for humanity—

the stream of the work of kosen-rufu began to
 push forth
from the unsparing effort
of one courageous man.
He stood up alone, decided in heart,
shadowed by the darkness, by the rain.

On May 3, 1951,
he said,
"If our goal of 750,000 households is not met
 before I die,
then cast my ashes into the sea off Shinagawa."
This thunderous declaration of his tore like a
 flame through the hearts of his comrades.

For the next seven years,
he took part in pitched battles, one after
 another,
never begrudging his life,
showing that we are supposed to fight only in
 the present moment:
Pouring your whole life into today's struggle
can bring out hundreds of thousands of years
 of value.

Ah, the days went by—
the waves of joy among friends awakened to
 their mission

pushed our ranks up to more than 750,000
 brave households
of Bodhisattvas of the Earth.

Nichiren Daishonin stood up seven hundred
 years ago.
Has the time turned ripe?
Or did we make and bring about the time?
How wondrous!
We have laid the foundation for kosen-rufu in
 the Latter Day of the Law.

Brought on by the heavenly deities,
or as a signal of Bonten and Taishaku
 descending from heaven,
it was said that our prime minister would come.
That day, March 16, declared our mentor,
would be a preliminary ceremony for kosen-rufu.

Youthful Bodhisattvas of the Earth
were the main performers in this grand
 ceremony.
On short notice, six thousand friends came
 together,
including the brass band members—
heroes of music for kosen-rufu.
Young angels of peace
in the fife and drum corps

adorned the stage with a magnificent and
 elegant march.

Together, in the hard chill of early morning,
we all savored the deliciousness of warm pork
 soup,
our mentor's generous spirit
warming our bodies and minds.
Shabbily got up,
but bursting with the pride and happiness
of living for a mission,
our joy in living along with our mentor
and in stepping forward together with him,
sparkled in smiles of the greatest satisfaction.

Without desire for either houses,
fame, wealth, or benefit of any kind,
our pure, brave spirit was all we possessed,
as we sought,
with our mentor,
to give up everything
for the sake of the great Law.
Only with that spirit and that resolve,
transcending life and death
to spread the Law,
were we able to bring about a history of perfect
 victory,
of moving on,
not giving in to any waves of devilish forces—
as the Daishonin writes in the Gosho.

Looking back,
on the morning of New Year's Day, 1958
stricken in his intense battle with the devil of
 illness,
our mentor told me his unquenchable desire:
"I want to fight for another seven years, to the
 reaching of a membership of two million
 households."
Feeling his longing,
my heart ached deep;
I resolved on that day
that I would take up the torch
for the winning of kosen-rufu,
and carry it successfully throughout my entire
 life, no matter what.

Many fellow comrades,
unaware of the severity of our mentor's illness,
remained hopeful about his recovery.
I alone,
having a long-range view of bringing about
 kosen-rufu in the future,
fixed my resolve deep in my heart,
never to forget his instructions, even in my
 sleep;
my mentor, too, telling me never to leave his
 side,
trained me wholeheartedly.

I will never forget his heartfelt desire:

"There is nothing more that I want.
All I hope for is capable people whom I can
 trust."

Ah, March 16.
The prime minister did not come,
but his wife and son-in-law came in his stead.
As the ceremonies opened,
despite his illness,
our mentor stood up bravely
at the head of this array of young Bodhisattvas
 of the Earth;
and there he passed on to us his great desire
 to accomplish kosen-rufu.

Mystically,
this hallowed event
became a solemn ceremony at which
the royal banner of succession was handed on
from mentor to disciple.

Our mentor, a father to us all,
ignoring his weakened body,
dared to determinedly take the lead.
A special litter was prepared by one of his
 disciples,
but he chided me:
"This is too big to head the whole assembly."
Yet he set himself on it, saying, "I will use it,

for you made it out of your sincerity";
in the depths of our lives, our understanding
 knew no bounds.

"No matter who may argue his success or
 failure,
truly he has given all he had to give
to the last moment of his life."

The figure of our mentor riding in the litter,
like the courageous bearing of K'ung-ming on
 the Wuchang Plain,
described in song,
casts a brilliant light that will shine forever.

The bold declaration of a hero without equal in
 the history of kosen-rufu—
"The Soka Gakkai is the king of the religious
 world"—
rang out through the gigantic, seven-hundred-
 year-old cedar trees.

For all posterity I want to set forth
his honorable triumph
as an uncrowned king of all humankind,
to sound over all the world
for the ten thousand years
of the Latter Day of the Law—
in significance, his pales even the great march

led by Alexander the Great.

His illness
was most serious;
wringing the last bit of energy from his life,
he uttered these words to me firmly as I
 heldhis arm:
"Now at last my work is complete.
I feel I am ready to die any time.
The rest will be up to you, Daisaku."
This still rings clear in my ears.

My mentor was then fifty-eight;
I, his disciple, was thirty.
Perhaps because he bequeathed to me long life,
for his sake, this year
I reached the milestone of sixty years of age.

You, young friends!
I ask
that you carry on in my footsteps
with the same heart as his.

Once, bedridden,
our mentor, who had carried out his mission
 undaunted,
having solemnly taken command of many fierce
 battles,
asked me,

"What book are you reading now?"
With his strict fatherly love
he urged me to study ever harder.
At another time,
he said with a warm look,
"I dreamt I went to Mexico....

"I will entrust world kosen-rufu to you."
Making his heart my own,
I swore to set out
for global kosen-rufu,
exactly as he had once written to me:
"As dynamically as a great eagle flying in the
 sky."

Only four days before his death,
he uttered these words: "Never let go your grip
 on our advancement, even if I should die."
Clear and severe, his words rang out like the
 roar of the lion king.
This directive became the mainstay for the
 fearless advance of his disciples.

Ah, unforgettable April 2.
In a cloud of cherry blossoms in the flush of
 full bloom,
our mentor went on to Eagle Peak;
but I, as part of his life,
boldly pushed off in a lifelong struggle

to drive on to the accomplishment of
 kosen-rufu.

At that time I wrote in my diary,
"A youth, a disciple of Toda, advances;
alone, he steadily plods ahead against the north
 wind."

Thirty years have passed since then.
Exposing myself to stormy winds,
enduring the broiling rays of the sun,
I stood firm, day after day,
and, to protect my dear fellow members,
I never budged even a step from facing up to
 every obstacle and devil.

Solemnly aware that
our victory stands for the truth of Buddhism,
I refused to hold back or to hesitate even a
 moment.
Amid the raging waves,
free of fear,
I showed
how a man of genuine courage must live.

During these past thirty years,
in a fearless and spirited way,
those dear brothers and sisters
who came together for our glorious March 16

have kept working on
in our never-regressing great march—
together with me
creating a splendid and victorious record of
 glory.

Before us
the storms of the three powerful enemies
rose up time and time again.
There were days
we faced waves of base attacks
and were betrayed by wickedly clever people.

Like the clear blue skies, however,
we have completely triumphed;
on the wings of hope,
we have overcome blizzards of hardships.

Young girls,
now queens enveloped by the golden breeze of
 happiness,
and young men,
now noble pillars of the great fortress of peace
 and humanity,
have magnificently laid out an unshakable
 foundation.
The power of unity—many in body, one in
 mind—
among members bound to one another

by mystic ties made up countless eons ago,
and the stern bonds of solidarity
dedicated to the ideals taught by the
 Daishonin—
both served as our diamond-like, indestructible
 axle to construct
the foundation for the kosen-rufu of the eternal
 future.

As an endless array of spirited youths arise
 today and tomorrow,
like white clouds hanging beyond the distant
 blue horizon,
and push off into the skies of the new century,
there will come no dark clouds of devils and
 obstacles;
The faces of those gallant youths,
children of the Buddha, will shine brilliantly,
and flower petals will dance in a waft of
 fragrant wind.

Youth is a priceless treasure;
every painful experience,
both victory and defeat,
becomes a launch for dramatic growth in the
future.
You, young friends,
call for another round of the Seven Bells!

Says a Buddhist principle: Buddhism will
 proceed eastward.
Buddhism came to Japan,
and then, seven hundred years later,
the great sage Nichiren Daishonin appeared like
 the sun.
Seven hundred years after his advent,
a wondrous group was born in Japan;
waves of propagation of the True Law,
now moving westward, began washing
the shores of Asia and of the world.
The Mystic Law, a great beacon to the dignity
 of life,
will shortly enwrap the entire blue earth.

Don't ask
Whether or not this mighty flow of kosen-rufu
will turn out to be a historical necessity.
Rather, always ask yourselves
whether or not you carry the passion of heart
to make kosen-rufu inevitable,
through your own sweat and toil.

Kosen-rufu calls for us
to make the flowers of the Renaissance of Life
bloom eternally all over this great earth,
as the supreme seat of the Buddha's life
is set up within the soul of all humanity,
exactly in accord with the Daishonin's will.

T'ien-t'ai states,
"From the indigo, an even deeper blue."
Something dyed with indigo comes out even
 bluer
than the indigo plant itself.

You too,
to your hearts' content,
chart a great course on the sea of history
to the victory of the people,
embracing the fundamental Law
that penetrates all things in the universe,
and drawing out infinite splendor from within
 your lives.
This is my constant prayer.

What promise did you make,
that you, courageous youths with a worthy
 mission,
are emerging in succession
now, at the start of the Era of Youth!

Ah!
Another great journey into the next thirty years
is about to start!

I believe
you will beautifully scale
unprecedented, rugged summits,

and proudly ring, again and again,
the bell of daybreak—
to usher in the new century.

The time has come around again
for us to observe Kosen-rufu Day.
This day signifies the dawn of hope
for my dear disciples.

Youth,
always push on.
Now is the time;
we should not go back even a step.

Youth,
sing the bright and brave song of youth
proudly and hopefully,
continuing to challenge your daily efforts
 courageously,
in your pursuit of study and training.

With a golden unity that will never break down,
give yourselves to accomplishing this,
our sacred undertaking,
bringing in a new day in the history of
 humankind.

With my deep prayer for the happiness and long lives of all those who gathered in the cold wind in the early morning hours of March 16, 1958.

March 9, 1988

***

Seven Bells: Successive seven-year periods that have marked the Soka Gakkai's advancement since its founding on November 18, 1930. May 3, 2001, marked the start of the second set of the Seven Bells, signaling the start of a new cycle in the SGI's history. The goal of the second set of Seven Bells (2001–50) is to secure the foundation for peace in Asia and throughout the world.

May 3: Designated "Soka Gakkai Day." May 3 is the anniversary of the inauguration of the Soka Gakkai's second and third presidents in 1951 and 1960, respectively. It is often used as a target date for advancing the movement of kosen-rufu.

"From the indigo, an even deeper blue": Nichiren, *The Writings of Nichiren Daishonin,* vol.1, 457. This simile is often used to indicate the disciple growing to surpass their mentor.

Unfurl the banner of youth

Ode to my young successors, our treasures of Soka

Let the intemperate winds
gust and rave!
Let the implacable waves
roil and rage!

I am young,
my youth a crimson banner
I unfurl against the wind.
I fear nothing,
succumb to nothing.

Here is the promontory
from which I depart,
today is my first campaign.
Gazing into my future
I feel ever-greater strength and courage
well forth from within!

Oh, wind and wave!
I will brave each harsh test unfazed

as a youth worthy of greatness!
My friend, set out on open oceans!
I will seek out vast new lands.

I will rise, come what may,
to take on a lifetime of struggles
of my own choosing.
With certainty I embark
knowing I possess
great purpose.

I am youth
eagerly flying
into the teeth of the storm.
Soaring—
on incandescent wings of freedom
to heights beyond those imagined
by any head of state, decrepit with age,
with more wisdom
than any cunning politician.

This is what it means
to occupy the imperishable
throne of youth.
Bearing in our hearts
the never-dimming star of destiny,
we shine.
To make the entire world our stage—
this is what it means

to be young.

Young people are humanity's treasure,
the great earth
from which peace springs.
When we come together in unity,
the thunder clap resounds
with an explosive roar,
admonishing
the arrogance of power.

Your sparkling eyes,
the vibrancy and dignity
that issues from your lives,
your limitless vitality
racing and running without end—
all this is the mark
of your hallowed, hope-filled soul.

No sorrow, anguish, or impediment
can slow you as you set out
for life's triumphal arch,
raising a cheerful toast
beneath the proudly fluttering
banner of victory
new and crimson.

I will forge on, come what may!
For this is clear proof

of youthful years
supremely spent
To what end? For what purpose?
In pursuit of those answers
I will battle on forever.

The night tormented by the storm's rage
—the night of billows that froth and spew—
inevitably yields to the day
as it breaks through eastern skies.
Confidently anticipating
that dawn, I forge on
again today.

I call upon youth,
I urge each of you:
with firmly grounded acumen,
be vigilant! raise your voice! charge forth!
Never forget:
Beyond the distant horizon
are those who will follow after,
who await the arrival of a light
whose source is as old and deep
as time itself.

Go now, my young friends,
set off on white steeds!
Gallop majestically, brilliantly!
Stand tall

in the front ranks of the people,
embracing your life's purpose
as the Buddha instructed.

Ascend mountains
traverse valleys;
ascend them with pleasure,
traverse them in wonder
together with a multitude
of kindred spirits.

Push on bravely
through the deepest dark.
Your prized labors, sweat, and toil
will lead you to the golden stage
of a new era
long dreamed of, yearned for.

My young friends!
Lift your sights, stand proud.
Take the lead in all things,
issue the loud clear call
of your very being and worth!

Young people
need never concede defeat—
for the refusal to give in
is in itself victory.

Young people need never kneel—
if your heart remains unbowed
in the face of any circumstance,
you will find
a glorious crown awaiting you.
Observe! Behold!
When I, a youth,
awaken and arise,
summoning forth my innermost strength,
a new era is invariably born,
and the dawn of revolution breaks!

A youth is one who can declare:
I am the eyes that reflect the future!
I am the fierce, eloquent flash of light
that reveals all truth
and exposes all lies,
the knife-edge of incisive justice
eternally stirring and rousing
human society...

May the gaze of the young gleam with hope!
May your hearts swell with energy and strength!

The waning century passes brutally.
Souls struggle in grief and dread,
writhe in the heavy remorse.
Dark recoiling of the century's end,
glowering clouds of chaos,

trembling before demonic weaponry.

The fracturing blasts of gunshot and bombs,
the screams of mothers and children
fleeing in desperation—
such are the notes and sounds
the decaying century
has splattered on its score.
To quote Beethoven:
"Oh friends, not these tones!"

It is the potent voices of youth in song
that will heal and restore
humanity's wounded history.

For this to be a truly new era
a truly new generation
must conduct the performance
of a magnificent music
that resounds through the cosmos.
Join me in song, my friend!
Share these solemn steps!
Let us dance together!

This sublime symphony
of young champions!
The grand prelude has already begun.

The bell has been struck!
Hoist sail!
Weigh anchor!
It is time for youth
wrapped in stars of glory,
to set out upon
this vast, unending journey!

My eternal comrades!
Are you fully prepared to win?
Pay meticulous heed to each detail,
for once you leave this rocky,
sheltering shore,
there is no turning back.

Leap like orcas breaching
upon the vast, expansive seas.
Feel the rolling of each massive wave
as the rocking of a cradle.
Never forget the inner fortitude
that brings triumph and success!

Each and every one of you!
Strive so that the many
—ally and adversary alike—
may all without exception
reach the far shores
of happiness and peace.

Step forward to become
the bow that slices
through wind and wave!
Serve as roaring engine
and driving propeller!
Work around the clock,
toiling in the engine room
though soot and grease
clog your every pore!
With joy and enthusiasm,
explore and pioneer your self.
Cross the tempest seas
in search of the untrod soil
of a new continent
dense with thick forests.
Reach those lands,
go boldly ashore!

Life is a struggle,
a battle lasting a lifetime.
This is a fact
we can neither deny nor avoid.

A proud and independent champion,
I wait for no one.
My heart is the site of ceaseless struggle,
a battlefield where fierce contests are waged—
the advance and retreat
of hope and despair,
courage and cowardice,

progress and stagnation.

No matter how bitter or deadening,
how harrowing or strained
my days may be,
I will advance one step
and then another,
until I break through
and open the path for all.

May you always heed these words:
"Nichiren's disciples cannot accomplish anything
if they are cowardly."
"Until kosen-rufu is achieved,
propagate the Law to the full extent of your
ability,
without begrudging your life."

Upholding these admonitions,
fight on with the noble spirit
of fearless heroes.

Young friends!
Because you are thoroughly versed
in profound philosophical truths,
you must never be fooled by impostors,
never mesmerized by their sorcery.
Unsheathe the blade of justice
until the last vicious oppressor

is brought low.

Let the winds of courage blow!
Daily strike this brazen bell!
Let the cry of our solidarity
reverberate in triumph!

Do not fear the howl of wolves!
Let them hear in turn the roar of lions!

In the midst of a defiled society
throw open the angry gates
and advance against those
who would upend what is right!
Let them know the strict severity
of endless regret!

Together let us win,
together spill tears of joy.
Never submit to those
who would bind our hearts with hypocrisy.

The pitched battles
in which youth engage
will invariably bring down
every last adversary of the Buddha.
Thus become
the effulgent sun

liberating people from fear!

In Hall Caine's masterwork,
Rossi and Bruno, two young comrades,
join each other's strengths in trust.
Undeterred by threat of execution
they struggle inseparably in order to build
"The Eternal City."

My young friends—
with an even greater comradeship
and unity of purpose,
succeed in constructing
an eternal city enduring over
the three realms of past, present, and future!
This is the meaning of kosen-rufu.

Until that day,
lock arms on shoulders
and advance!

There are thousands, tens of thousands,
of young people who embrace
the same ideals of peace
awaiting you in the United States!
Thousands, ten thousands more
great comrades await
in Latin and Central America;
in Europe as well!

In Africa, Asia, and Oceania!

Join hands
—freely, fully—
with all the world's youth!
Set your feet and move as one.
Build the Eternal City of the Twenty-first
 Century
adamantine and indestructible!

*In commemoration of July 3
the day Josei Toda was released from prison
the day I was imprisoned*

***

Written on June 10, 1998, to commemorate
July 3, the day the author was detained on
false charges in 1957. On the same day in
1945, his mentor, Josei Toda, was released
from prison where he had been incarcerated
by Japan's wartime military government. This
translation, by the Soka Gakkai, first appeared
in *Journey of Life* (2014).

"Oh friends, not these tones!": Translated from
Beethoven, "An die Freude" (Ode to Joy) in
Symphonien Nr 6–9, 195.

"Nichiren's disciples": Nichiren, *The Writings of Nichiren Daishonin,* vol.1, 481.

"Until kosen-rufu is achieved": Translated from Nichiren, *Nichiren Daishonin gosho zenshu,* 1618.

Hall Caine's masterwork: Caine, *The Eternal City.*

May the fragrant laurels of happiness adorn your life

Dedicated to my beloved young women's division members

How beautiful is the sun,
its limitless, multihued lights revealing
the inherent dignity of humankind!
This undeniable force,
this unfaltering existence dedicated
to fulfilling its vow,
to illuminating all things for all time!

In the presence of the sun
there is no darkness.
In the presence of the sun
there is no discrimination.

In the presence of the sun
the same rights are shared by all
and a world of peace shines brightly.

Today once more

I will walk my chosen path
pursue my chosen work
bring my history to new luster.
Undeterred by deceitful rains,
I will walk a path of bright smiles
true to myself, as only I can,
undefeated by anything!
For I understand this path
to be my treasured way.

Youth—
this time in life that comes but once,
dignified and precious
like a glittering gem.
I will live vivaciously, with all my might
Because to do is to lay the foundations
of a lifetime,
and from here is born a new happiness
arising from the very core of my being.

I will never stop advancing!
Even in the face of great difficulties

I will not turn back.
Life must be lived—
strongly, honestly, cheerfully!

Of course there will be bad times
along with the good.

But I will never hurl insults at life.

The growing vital force that is youth—
in each joyous stride
there is so much to read and learn
so much wisdom to seek.

Whatever the blizzards of this life
you can emerge triumphant
by the strengths residing
within your heart.

What a joyful prospect—
to live each day of youth
with wisdom, savoring happiness
and meaningful hope
in a world peopled with beautiful hearts!

In such a life,
everything you undergo
forms a garland crown
of woven flowers
that adorns your brow.

Daughter of unfathomable mission!
You transform the ashen winter landscape
into a vivid dance of spring
bathed in soft sunlight.

I will not lose my footing
in the morass of society.
I feel no envy for the illusory shadows
of glamour and fame.
Nor am I shaken by heartless criticism.

For I embrace principles
that are eternal
and merit my complete faith.
I have my SGI family—
sisters who share my aspirations,
who are trustworthy
and with whom I can share anything.

The inner vitality of youth
bright as the morning sun
holds all the world's wealth of gold.
To be young, in itself,
is to inhabit a castle of jewels.

The palace of your life sparkles
with the light of gems more numerous
than the stars filling the heavens.

Nothing could be more sublime
than this treasure possessed by all.
No one in this world is better than others.
We are all equally, ordinarily human.

In his later years
the world-acclaimed violinist
Yehudi Menuhin declared:
God resides with our hearts.
Likewise, the Buddha is found
within our lives,
not in temples or monasteries.

This treasure is something
that no one can take from you
for it *is* you, you yourself.
To awaken to this fact
is happiness.

Just as the lamp you light for another
will illuminate your own way,
the heart that desires the happiness of others
will be filled with the bright starlight
of happiness.

My joy is not confined
within a narrow room.
There is space for all to enter,
for this friend and that.

The forces of selfish ego
work to drive others out,
to gain sole possession
of the jeweled chamber.

Such people end up
banished from their own palace,
left to wander in hellish solitude.

The warm camaraderie
of friends joined hand in hand,
like endless vistas of floral garlands,
multiplies my joy many times over.

"Kindness is the flower of strength,"
said José Martí, hero of Cuban independence.

As a flower that blooms proudly
despite the pelting rains,
I will share this smile
with my friends and companions!

If you are cowardly or weak
you cannot offer others protection.
In the end, you'll be left facing
your most pitiable, compassionless self.

Only by triumphing over your own sorrow
can you fully feel the dark misery
afflicting a friend.
Only when you win over your own weakness
can you ease the troubles of others.

Be strong! Ever strong!
These are the crucial watchwords
that open the doors
to the palace of happiness.
Bid farewell to songs of sadness.
Triumph over inner weakness.
Reject self-deception
and come to know yourself
as someone who never betrays
what is true and just!

Faith is not emotionalism or self-pity;
it is about winning in your life!

Daughter with sparkling eyes!
Your youth alone makes you
a princess of happiness!
Soar high above the
sinister anguished clouds!
Stretch wide the wings of freedom
propelled by the vibrant force
of your spirit!
Gaze down from those heights
on festering swamps of envy!

You must never submit
to forlornly swaying emotions.
Maintain your pride and dignity!
Direct your heart with

firmness and certainty!

Always remember
you are a monarch of humanity!
Maintain regal focus
on a treasured throne
enveloped in a world
of rich colors and varied lights!

Nichiren Daishonin instructs us
to be the masters of our minds
and not let our minds be our masters.
These words are an eternal beacon
to light your life's journey.

In my heart—
the flame of an imperishable philosophy burns
the light of lifetime purpose shines
magnificent goals reside.

Those whose hearts are set
on profound and focused prayer
are freed from hesitancy.
They do not fear
the aimless drifting into darkness.
In the depths of their being
a bright, untrammeled path
of peace and contentment
unfolds without end.

I will not drown in the
illusory images of renown
as they shimmer fleetingly
on the water's surface!

Make companions
of the sun and the moon
as they shine with undying light!

Take joy in quiet striving
on the ground of daily living.
Live out your life in its actuality
—in the midst of reality—
advancing always toward happiness!

Noble young women!
Do not cling to trivial things!
For the foolish find themselves living
far from the realm of heavenly beings.
They will be carried off by angry, roaring waves.

Never be deceived or taken in!
There is not the slightest need
to be jealous
of anyone else!

Only you know the reality
of your own life.

The scorn of others
based on their personal perception
is nothing more than that.
Live true to yourself—
those who do
are happy.

If you are wise and clear-sighted
you have already attained
a life of magnificent victory.
I possess the mirror
of pristine life
that reflects with unsparing clarity
the evil of this world—
a life that, like the pure white lotus,
remains unsullied
amidst the dirt and dust
of a squalid age!
I possess the jewel-encrusted
sword of an idealism that makes
the corrupt and unscrupulous
tremble in shame!

Fresh new flower of revolution!
Joan of Arc for the coming era!
With your silvery voice
you reinvigorate
the sleepy veterans
of past campaigns;
you inspire courage in the hearts

of a fatigued generation
spurring them
to rise and fight again.

History recounts
that Joan of Arc
was just an ordinary girl.
But the people of the village
where she lived described her
as a young woman of initiative.

She willingly worked,
she readily spun,
she gladly pulled the plow...
And when the time came,
she took the lead
to fight and rescue
France from peril!

The curtain is now rising
on the grand stage
of the twenty-first century!
The time has come
for the daughters of the sun
crowned with laurels
to take the lead
to move with vibrant
grace and courage!

A fresh breeze blows
and the pure blue sky
stretches into eternity.
So let us spread our wings!
Rise dancing bravely into the sky,
fly with flaming hope
into the future that awaits
in the vast new century
that is yours.

Daughters of the sun!
Always remember
the noble mothers and fathers
who worked selflessly
braving wind and rain
to build this Soka castle
of value creation!

March 24, 1999

***

Written for the members of the Soka Gakkai
young women's division. This translation, by
the Soka Gakkai, first appeared in *Journey of
Life* (2014).

"Kindness is the flower of strength": Translated from Martí, *Amistad Funesta* (Fatal Friendship) in *Obras Completas,* vol.18, 198.

José Martí (1853–95): Cuban poet, journalist, and revolutionary philosopher known as the "Apostle of Cuban Independence."

Glossary

bodhisattva One who aspires to enlightenment, or Buddhahood, and carries out altruistic practices. It also indicates a state of life characterized by compassion. The bodhisattva ideal is central to the Mahayana Buddhist tradition as the individual who seeks happiness both for him- or herself and for others.

Bodhisattvas of the Earth An innumerable host of bodhisattvas who emerge from beneath the earth as described in "Emerging from the Earth," the 15th chapter of the Lotus Sutra. The Buddha, Shakyamuni, entrusts to them the task of propagation of the essence of the Lotus Sutra in the time after his death. Nichiren regarded those who embrace and propagate the teaching of the Mystic Law as Bodhisattvas of the Earth.

Buddha Literally "Awakened One"; one who perceives the true nature of all life and who leads others to attain the same enlightenment. The Buddha nature or condition of Buddhahood exists within all beings and is characterized by the qualities of wisdom, courage, compassion, and life force. Historically this indicates Shakyamuni, the founder of Buddhism.

Buddhism of the sun Indicates the Buddhism of Nichiren Daishonin established in 1253.

daimoku The practice of chanting Nam-myoho-renge-kyo with belief in the fundamental Law of the universe expounded by Nichiren. See Nam-myoho-renge-kyo.

Daishonin See Nichiren.

Dharma The teachings or universal law of enlightenment taught by the Buddha.

eight winds Eight conditions that prevent people from advancing along the path to enlightenment. They are prosperity, decline, disgrace, honor, praise, censure, suffering, and pleasure.

Gohonzon The scroll that serves as the object of devotion in Nichiren Buddhism. SGI members chant Nam-myoho-renge-kyo to a Gohonzon enshrined in their own homes in order to bring forth the life state of Buddhahood from within.

Great Law Indicates the Dharma. See Mystic Law.

heavenly deities The Buddhist gods or benevolent deities that protect the correct Buddhist teaching and its practitioners. Forces in life that function to protect the people and their land and bring good fortune to both.

human revolution The term used by Josei Toda to describe a fundamental process of inner transformation whereby individuals can unleash the full potential of their lives and take control over their own destiny.

kosen-rufu A Japanese phrase literally meaning "to declare and spread widely." It refers to the process of securing lasting peace and happiness for all humankind by establishing the humanistic ideals of Nichiren Buddhism in society. Kosen-rufu is often used synonymously with world peace, and more broadly could be understood as a vision of social peace brought about by the widespread acceptance of core values such as unfailing respect for the dignity of human life.

Lotus Sutra Widely recognized as one of the most important and influential sutras, or sacred scriptures, of Buddhism, forming the core of the Mahayana school. In the sutra, Shakyamuni reveals that all people can attain enlightenment and that Buddhahood—a condition of absolute happiness, freedom from fear and from all illusions—is inherent in all life.

Mystic Law The ultimate law, principle, or truth of life and the universe in Nichiren's teachings; the Law of Nam-myoho-renge-kyo.

Nam-myoho-renge-kyo An invocation established by Nichiren on April 28, 1253. The title of the Lotus Sutra in its Japanese translation is Myoho-renge-kyo. To Nichiren, Nam-myoho-renge-kyo was the expression, in words, of the law of life that all Buddhist teachings seek to clarify. Practitioners of Nichiren Buddhism chant Nam-myoho-renge-kyo as their core Buddhist practice. This is sometimes described as chanting daimoku.

Nichiren (1222–82) A Buddhist reformer who lived in thirteenth-century Japan, often referred to by the honorific title "Daishonin" or "great sage." His intensive study of the Buddhist sutras convinced him that the Lotus Sutra contained the essence of the Buddha's enlightenment and that it held the key to transforming people's suffering and enabling the peaceful flourishing of society. Nichiren established the invocation of Nam-myoho-renge-kyo in 1253. His claims invited an onslaught of often violent persecutions from the military government and the established Buddhist schools. Throughout, he refused to compromise his principles to appease those in authority.

Soka Gakkai Literally "Value Creation Society," a Japanese lay Buddhist movement based on the practice of Nichiren Buddhism, founded in 1930 by Tsunesaburo Makiguchi and Josei Toda. Originally called Soka Kyoiku Gakkai (Value-Creating Education Society), it expanded rapidly in postwar Japan to become one of the world's largest lay Buddhist movements.

Soka Gakkai International (SGI) Founded by Daisaku Ikeda in 1975, a worldwide network of lay Buddhists dedicated to a shared vision of a better world through the empowerment of the individual and the promotion of peace, culture, and education based upon the teachings of Nichiren.

Shakyamuni (Gautama Siddhartha) Also known as the Buddha or Awakened One. The historical founder of Buddhism. Born in what is now Nepal some 2,500 years ago, he renounced his royal upbringing to embark on a spiritual quest to understand how human suffering could be ended. While in deep meditation, he experienced a profound awakening, or enlightenment. He then traveled throughout the Indian subcontinent sharing his enlightened wisdom, promoting peace, and teaching people how to unleash the great potential of their lives. The Lotus Sutra is said to contain his ultimate teaching: the universal possibility of enlightenment.

three existences Past existence, present existence, and future existence. Used to indicate all of time from the eternal past, through the present, and into the eternal future. In Buddhism, the three existences represent the three aspects of the eternity of life, linked inseparably by the inner law of cause and effect.

three thousand realms contained in a single life moment A doctrine developed by the Great Teacher T'ien-t'ai of China based on the Lotus Sutra. The principle, usually referred to as three thousand realms in a single moment of life, means that all phenomena are contained within a single moment of life, and that a single moment of life permeates the three thousand realms of existence, or the entire phenomenal world.

Toda, Josei (1900–58) An educator, publisher, and entrepreneur who became the second president of the Soka Gakkai and the mentor of Daisaku Ikeda. Along with Tsunesaburo Makiguchi (the founding president of the Soka Gakkai who was imprisoned along with Josei Toda and who later died in prison), Mr. Toda was incarcerated during World War II for his criticism of the government's wartime policies. After the war, he rebuilt the Soka Gakkai into a dynamic popular movement with members throughout Japan.

treasure tower A massive tower or stupa adorned with treasures or jewels described in the eleventh chapter of the Lotus Sutra. It indicated the enormity, profundity, and dignity of both the universal Law of life, Nam-myoho-renge-kyo, and individuals who inherently possess the Law within their lives.

True Law Indicates the Dharma. See Mystic Law.

CPSIA information can be obtained
at www.ICGtesting.com
Printed in the USA
BVHW010226040619
550095BV00006B/77/P

9 781525 272943